HAWAIIAN REFLECTIONS

Today, one of the deepest needs of
mankind is the need to feel a sense
of kinship with one another . . .

HAWAIIAN REFLECTIONS

by Rick Golt

Produced and published by
Mutual Publishing Co.
P. O. Box 3793
Honolulu, Hawaii 96812

INTRODUCTION

This is a very personal book. It is a series of reflections, momentary impressions of Hawaii. Each is separate, an entity to itself. Yet they are not separate; to me they are all part of what makes Hawaii unique. I think that trying to explain it further would be unfair. The real reflection is in the eye and the mind of the reader - therein lies its personal meaning.

The photographs were made throughout the islands over a period of years. I made them because they seemed meaningful of the spirit that is the magic of Hawaii. They are but a few brief glimpses into the myriad worlds and peoples who for me are Hawaii.

The quotations in this book have been gathered over a period of years, and from many sources. I have combined them with the photographs in a manner that for me created an interrelationship. In each case, that relationship is different . . . yet in all cases I feel that something of a further entity of its own identity was created.

Every effort has been made to assure the accuracy of the quotations. A great number of these have been verified with the assistance of the editors of Bartlett's *Familiar Quotations.* Their assistance is most appreciated.

In my seemingly endless trampings of the islands in my work, many people have been kind to me and believed in what I was doing. Without their help and consideration I would never have found many of the places and things, people and meanings that have gone into this work. More importantly, I never would have grown slowly to see, understand and appreciate something of the many ways of life that make Hawaii what it is. To all of these people I owe my deepest appreciation. To them I am continually grateful. But above all, I am thankful to my beloved Piggy, who has always been patiently at my side, trying to understand . . . and always believing.

Rick Golt
Honolulu
March 1978

Man's need for some degree of beauty
and serenity becomes more desperate
as our lives become more complex.

Aaron Levine, Oahu Development Conference

E malama ʻIa Na pono
o ka ʻaina e na ʻopio.

The ways of the people
are kept alive by its youth.

God, I thank thee
that I am not as other men are . . .

Luke 18:11

Truth is revealed in communication.
Perfect communication is achieved in silence.

SK Majumadar

Courage is
doing what you're afraid to do . . .

Eddie Rickenbacker

May you live all the days of your life.

Johnathan Swift

Man's capacities
have never been measured:
nor are we able to judge what he can do
by any precedents.
So little has been tried.

H. D. Thoreau

The meaning of life here on earth
might be defined as consisting in this:
to unfold yourself,
to work what thing you have the faculty for.
It is a necessity for the human being,
the first law of our existence.

Thomas Carlyle

The mind of man is capable of anything—
because everything is in it,
all the past as well as all the future.

Joseph Conrad

Music is the universal language of mankind . . .

Henry Wadsworth Longfellow

The business of the samurai consists
in reflecting on his own station in life,
in discharging loyal service to his master
if he has one,
in deepening his fidelity
in associations with friends,
and, with due consideration
of his own position,
in devoting himself to the duty above all.

Yamaga Soko *The Way of the Samurai*

There is no duty we so much underrate
as the duty of being happy.

Robert Louis Stevenson

Life was meant to be lived,
and curiosity must be kept alive.
One must never,
for whatever reason,
turn his back to life.

Anna Eleanor Roosevelt

When you cannot find peace in yourself
it is useless to look for it elsewhere.

La Rochefoucauld

What you think of yourself
is much more important
than what others
think of you.

Seneca

That so few now dare to be eccentric marks the chief danger of the time.

John Stuart Mill

I do not love him because he is good,
but because he is my little child.

Rabindranath Tagore

How many mountains,
how many rivers are still to be crossed
before I gain the land
where loneliness comes to an end?
Today, as ever, I travel on.

Wakayama Bokusui

The scars of others should teach us caution.

St. Jerome

The great end of life is not knowledge,
but action.

Thomas Henry Huxley

Na wai ho‘i ka‘ ole o ke akamai,
he alanui i ma‘a i ka hele
‘ia e o‘u mau makua?

Who would not be wise
on the path so long walked upon
by my ancestors?

Liholiho, Kamehameha IV

To me, old age
is always fifteen years older than I am.

Bernard Baruch

All the flowers of all the tomorrows
are in the seeds of today.

Chinese Proverb

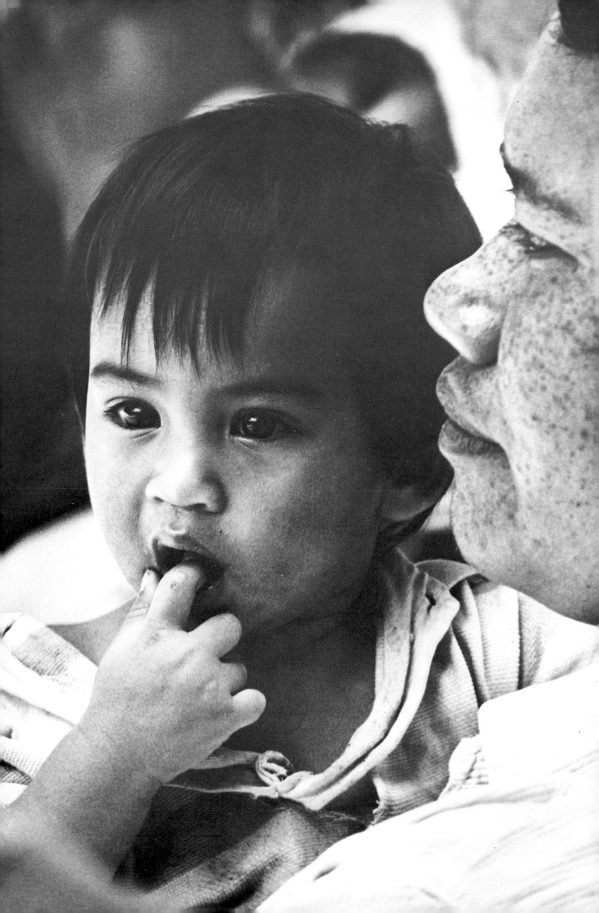

Everyone sits in the prison of his own ideas.

Albert Einstein

. . . a generation fails of its human promise
when it merely conserves the old.

Dr. Thomas Hale Hamilton

Man is the only animal that laughs and weeps;
for he is the only animal that is struck
by the difference between what things are
and what they might have been.

William Hazlitt

One of the great secrets of success
is to find a way of doing something,
rather than a reason why it can't be done . . .

Bud Smyser, Editor, *Honolulu Star Bulletin*

Force has no place
where there is need of skill.

Herototus

When we build,
let us think that we build forever.

John Ruskin

Risk! Risk! Care no more
for the opinion of others,
or for those voices.
Do the hardest thing on earth for you.
Act for yourself.
Face the truth.

Katherine Mansfield

There is no remedy for love
but to love more.

Henry David Thoreau

If one live a hundred years idle,
without energy,
better to live one day of steadfast energy.

Suttapitaka

Bitter are the tears of a child;
Sweeten them.
Deep are the thoughts of a child;
Quiet them.
Sharp is the grief of a child;
Take it from him.
Soft is the heart of a child;
Do not harden it.

Lady Wyndham Glenconner

No one knows what he can do till he tries.

Publilius Syrus

To know, to think, to dream.
That is everything.

Victor Hugo

Inaction in a dynamic world
is not only unnatural,
it is disastrous.

William F. Quinn, Address to Legislature of Hawaii

There are two things in life:
first, to get what you want;
and second,
after that to enjoy it.
Only the wisest of mankind
achieve the second.

Logan Pearsall Smith

A good man
doubles the length of his existence.
To have lived so as to look back with pleasure
is to have lived twice.

Martial

Nothing great
was ever achieved without enthusiasm.

Ralph Waldo Emerson

Love comforteth like sunshine after rain.

William Shakespeare

Love consists in this,
that two solitudes protect
and touch and greet each other.

Rainer Maria Rilke

Nothing will ever be attempted
if all possible objections
must first be overcome.

Samuel Johnson

A secret between two is a secret of God;
a secret among three is everybody's secret.

French Proverb

A truly great man
never puts away the simplicity of a child.

Chinese Proverb

We owe it to our ancestors
to preserve those human rights
which they have delivered to our care.
We owe it to posterity
not to permit their most precious inheritance
to be destroyed.

"Junius" to the *London Public Advertiser,* 1769

Cultural interchange has definite practical
aspects in promoting peace and stability.

Chancellor Howard P. Jones

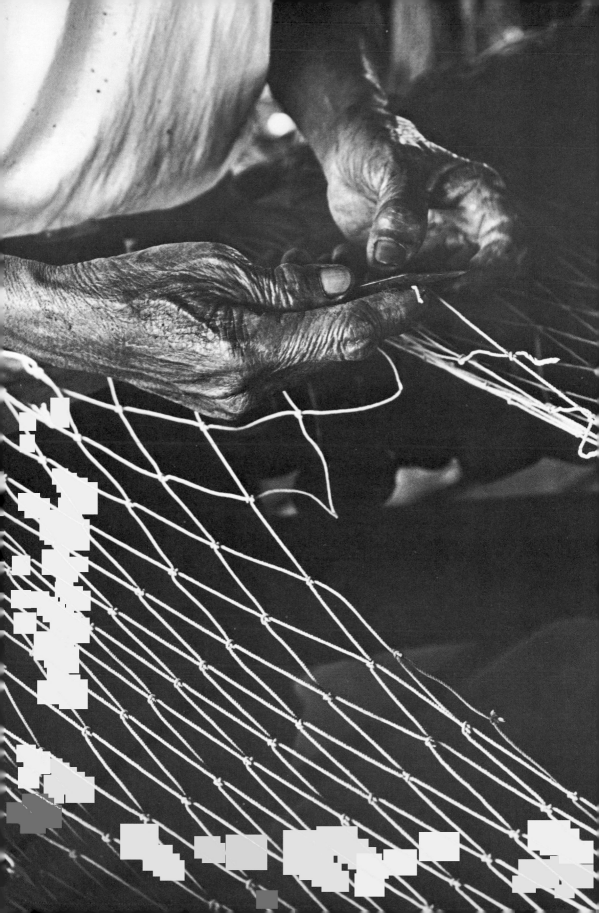

Work is love made visible.

Kahlil Gibran

Ah, but a man's reach
should exceed his grasp,
or what's a heaven for?

Robert Browning

Execute every act of thy life
as though it were thy last.

Marcus Aurelius

The eyes of Young Hawaii
may dream of a romantic past,
but they must devine a realistic future.
The new generation's heritage is faith;
its horizon is hope . . .

A. Grove Day, Senior Professor of English, University of Hawaii

Every day I remind myself that my life
is based on the labors of other men,
living and dead,
and that I must exert myself in order to
give in the same measure as I receive.

Albert Einstein

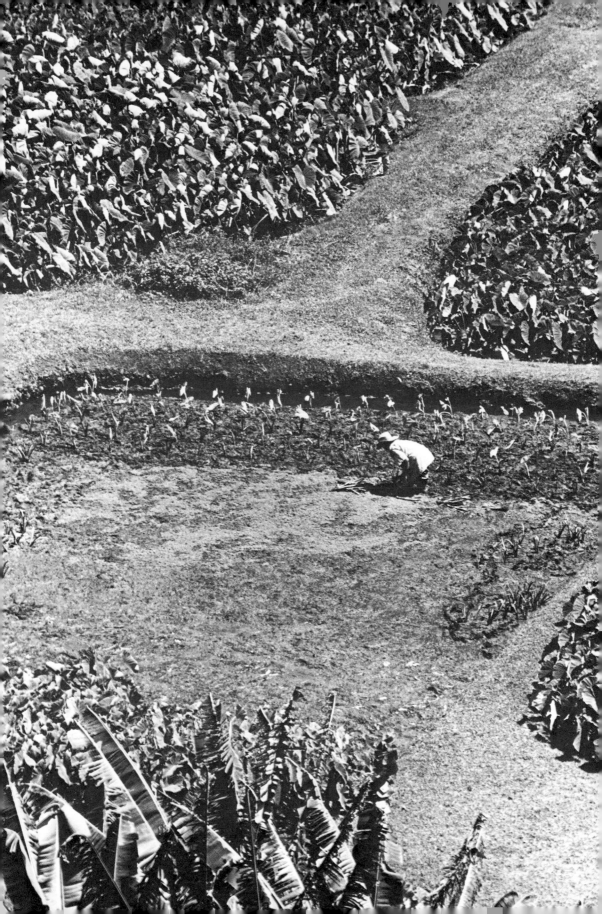

A peace above all earthly dignities,
A still and quiet conscience.

William Shakespeare

NOTES ON PHOTOGRAPHS

Over many years I have done a great deal of wandering. I go out with a camera and a few lenses in a bag and wander around looking for something that seems important. I suppose my purpose is to actually find something, although at times just the wandering gives the same feeling. A great deal goes on in the world, so one really need not wander far. When I happen upon something that seems important to me, I begin to photograph it. I continue to photograph it until it no longer seems important to keep photographing it. Then I wander on . . .

That, in brief, is how the photographs in this book came into being. I wandered the back streets and roads, beaches and mountains of the islands with my camera. Thousands upon thousands of things have seemed important and I have photographed them. It's a fatiguing sort of search, for I never quite know what I will come upon at the next turn. I do know, however, that it may be something tremendously important and I cannot relax my attention. Thus I wander around with my eyes and brain tuned to the "visual mode," looking for something yet unknown and unseen, subconsciously always evaluating what I am seeing. Thus, also, it is that I often walk past friends without a word when my eyes and brain are elsewhere, ahead of my body.

Often I wish that I were invisible. This would give me a tremendous advantage in the sort of work that is in this book. To me photography is simply an abstraction of life. It is vital therefore that if a photograph is going to succeed in interpreting and conveying what I have seen, that it originate from a totally natural and real life situation. I never could pose such a photograph. It simply wouldn't mean anything - to me, or to anyone else.

All of these photographs are glimpses into another person's life and world. They were made in the most candid sense, totally without any awareness on the part of the subject. Even the photographs of someone looking directly into the lens are done at a moment of recognition, when the subject was still on the verge of realizing my presence. That infinitely brief moment passes in a blink and is the last possible glimpse of reality. From that instant, the situation dissolves and vanishes. When my presence is known, a new reality forms; the reality that I was photographing has disappeared forever. Then is when I wander on my way . . . wishing I could be invisible.

The photographs were made with existing light. I adjust myself and my camera to make this light work for my intended purpose in the photograph. The same applies to composition and form, angle and area. I put all my effort into working all of these things together until they are in the right place at the same time. Then - and only then - do I have the very essence of the photograph at hand.

There is a sort of constant progression that I go through to arrive at this point. I photograph at all angles, carefully moving in and out, almost hypnotized as though I were watching a snake, all the time studying what is unfolding in front of me in real life and trying to adapt myself to it, always shifting for various alternatives. Sometimes this relationship continues for many minutes and I make many photographs. Often it ends in the flash of an eye: I am discovered . . . or a terribly important scene simply breakes up and dissolves.

In my work I tend to prefer dark prints. There is something about large areas of black that leave a great deal to the imagination of the viewer. Yet there seems to be a far greater and immediate impact in a strong dark image. Somehow the significance and meaning are more closely defined and understandable in that print. There is something of a greater symbolic and graphic quality in a darker print, something that more readily strikes the senses. I simply prefer it.

My overall feeling is that photography is life. Be it symbolic, interpretative or documentary, the photograph is merely a visual comment on life itself. The degree to which it succeeds is determined by the photographer at the release of the shutter. That is his obligation, his curse and his reward . . .

Rick Golt

RICK GOLT

Born in 1937, Rick Golt came to photography through the traditional arts. After graduating from Miami University in Ohio, and putting in a stint as a Navy pilot, he turned his efforts to painting, etching and writing his way through Europe for several years.

Over thirteen years ago, he came upon a photographic art show in the Stedelijk museum in Amsterdam, and was so deeply impressed that he took up the camera as his new-found artistic brush.

Since then, he has been an advertising creative director, published numerous photographic books, had the first major one man photographic shows in Hawaii - from the Contemporary Arts Center to the Academy of Art. His work has been widely recognized as innovative in the forms of photographic art. Today he has photographs and murals in a great number of private and corporate collections - as well as museums - throughout the Pacific, United States and Europe.